PEMBROKESHIRE LIMEKILNS

LIMEKILNS AND LIME BURNING AROUND THE PEMBROKESHIRE COAST

"A man doth sand for himself, lime for his son
and marl for his grandchild."
Old Pembrokeshire saying

PETER B. S. DAVIES

MERRIVALE

All rights reserved. No part of this publication may be reproduced, stored in a retrieval system or transmitted in any form or by any means electronic, photocopying, recording or otherwise, without the prior permission of the author.

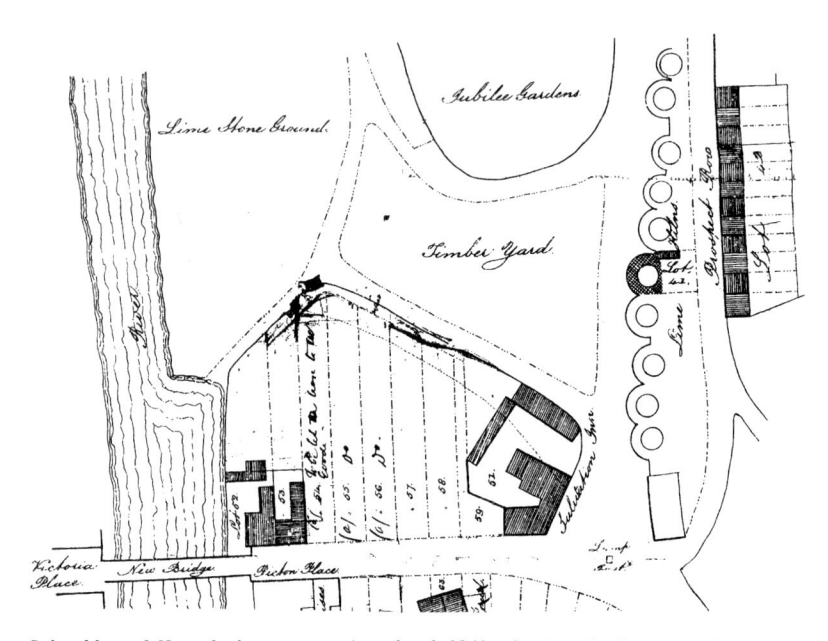

Sales Map of Haverfordwest properties, dated 1840, showing the layout of the Cartlett limekilns at that time.

Copyright: Peter B. S. Davies 1997

First Published 1989 under the Title
DEWISLAND LIMEKILNS (ISBN 0 9515207 0 9)
Second (Revised and Enlarged) Edition 1997

ISBN 0 9515207 7 6

Acknowledgements

I wish to express my grateful thanks to members of staff of the following institutions for their help and guidance and for permission to study various maps and documents in their collections: Haverfordwest Record Office; Haverfordwest Reference Library; National Library of Wales, Aberystwyth; Royal Commission for Ancient Monuments, Aberystwyth

My thanks are due to Roy Lewis and Robert Nisbet for providing additional information on North Pembrokeshire and Haverfordwest and to Les Owen who kindly supplied details of the Bristol Bills of Entry. I am particularly grateful to David James and George Harries for their generous advice and support at all times.

For permission to reproduce illustrations included in the present edition I wish to thank the following: National Library of Wales, Aberystwyth, (10); Desmond Hampson, (12); Gerald Oliver, (13); also Haverfordwest Record Office, (sales maps and bills). Finally, I wish to thank Olwen Griffiths for allowing me to quote from *Looking Back*, which was written by her father, John Miles Thomas.

Published by Merrivale, St. David's
Printed by C.I.T., Haverfordwest

Cover: Limekilns at Solva Harbour.

Coastal Limekilns of Pembrokeshire

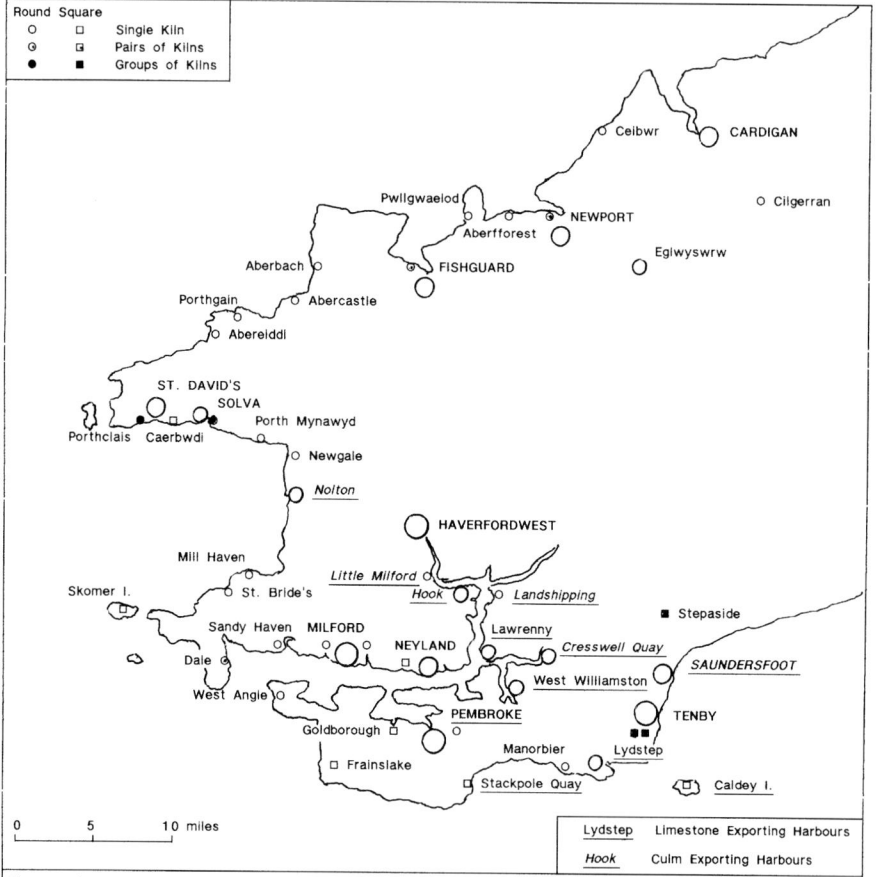

Round	Square	
O	□	Single Kiln
⊙	▫	Pairs of Kilns
●	■	Groups of Kilns

Lydstep — Limestone Exporting Harbours
Hook — Culm Exporting Harbours

The map shows locations on or near the Pembrokeshire Coast Path where reasonably well preserved limekilns are to be seen. Remains of kilns are also to be found elsewhere, particularly around the shores of Milford Haven. Sites of inland kilns are, with a few exceptions, not marked.

1. The massive square limekiln at Caerbwdi, once the property of the Bishop.

Contents

I	Sentinels by the Shore	7
II	Friends of Agriculture	9
III	An Ancient Industry	15
IV	The Years of Prosperity	22
V	The Silent Sentinels	36
	Pembrokeshire Limekilns; a Selection	44
	Bibliography	48

The Limekilns of Dewisland

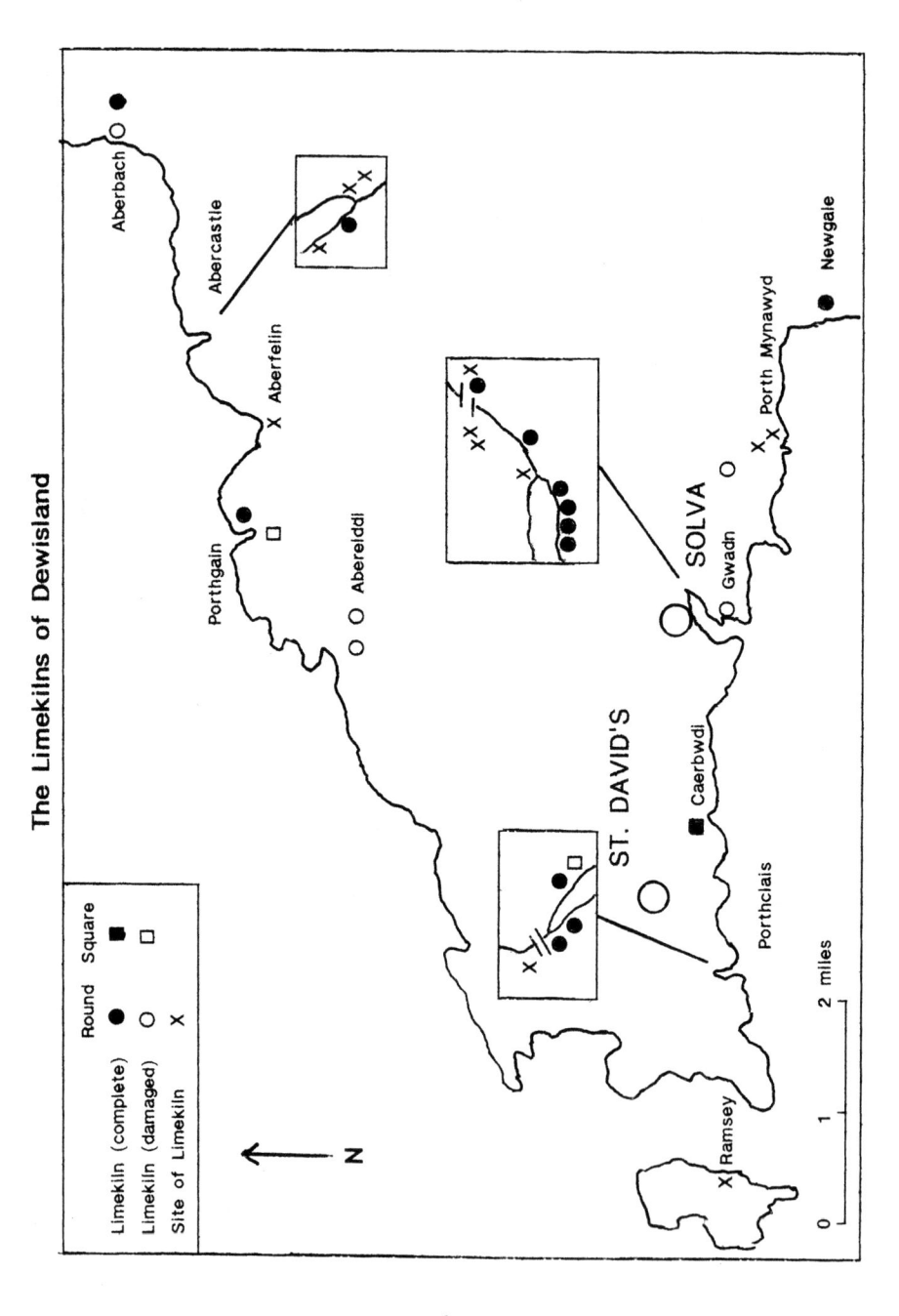

I; Sentinels by the Shore

The tiny cove of Caerbwdi, barely a mile from St. David's, is one of the secret gems of the Pembrokeshire coast. Its solitary claim to fame is that from these cliffs came the beautiful purple-red sandstone of which the cathedral is built.

A grassy lane, its banks resplendent with golden gorse and purple heather, leads down to a secluded and unspoilt bay. The narrow, boulder-strewn valley is a place of silence, save only for the chatter of the brook below as it tumbles headlong over the stones.

Yet, once, men lived and worked here. Beside the stream are the crumbling grey stone walls of what was Caerbwdi Mill. Beyond is what Fenton would have called a 'Friend of Agriculture', one of the limekilns which were so vital to the local economy.

Nearly twenty feet square and over twelve feet high, it is built into the hillside. Two fireplaces, one on either side, the 'kiln eyes' stare sightlessly across the valley, while the circular crucible is overgrown with brambles. Thanks to its sturdy construction it has stood the ravages of time far better than the nearby mill.

Not only the farmer depended on the limekilns. They were as essential to Abraham Rees, who was miller here in the last century, as to Henry Rees who farmed Carnwchwrn.

Others had reason to be grateful to them. Indirectly they provided work for the quarrymen of Pembroke and West Williamston, and for the miners of Hook and Nolton. Henry Grinnis, master of the sloop *Kitty*, and his crew were among those who brought in culm and limestone from South Pembrokeshire, and carried out the corn which merchants like George Williams exported to Bristol.

Some were more directly dependent on the kilns. There were the carters who carried the lime from kiln to field, and farm workers who spread it on the ground until it glistened like snow, and they were as white as the land.

Lastly there was the limeburner himself; a John y Galchen (John the limestone) who probably lived in the hovel beside the kiln. The name describes him; a ghostly pale figure flitting through the grey mist that rose from the fiery crucible of the kiln.

All have long gone, but for the farmer and a few agricultural workers. Now they spread artificial fertilizers instead of lime. Road transport has taken over from the coastal trader, and merchants come from afar to purchase the early potatoes for which Pembrokeshire is today famed. The kilns are cold, and the trade of limeburner is but a distant memory.

The relics of the industry are still to be seen in the limekilns which are such a prominent feature of the Pembrokeshire landscape. In the south of the county they are to be found in large numbers along the line of the limestone deposits. Others are scattered along the entire coast of the county and around the shores of Milford Haven. The 1906 Ordnance Survey map shows over 250 kilns, but many others had already disappeared.

The largest surviving kilns are to be found in the south of the county; at Kiln Park, just south of Tenby, are two groups, each consisting of six kilns which are some 30 feet high. They are situated at the old Blackrock limestone quarries and at one time were served by railway sidings. At Stepaside is another group, built in the nineteenth century to provide lime used (at that time) for removing acidic impurities from the iron ore being smelted at the local ironworks.

They were the exceptions. Most of the kilns in the south of the county were small, often they were set up by individual farmers in the corners of fields, and burnt limestone quarried nearby. The culm was brought by horse and cart from mines only a few miles distant. By now the great majority have been demolished or lie crumbling, overgrown and forgotten.

Each of the major harbours along the Pembrokeshire coast had its complement of kilns. In 1887 there were four in Fishguard, including two (which still survive) at the Slade; however an early nineteenth century drawing shows half a dozen in that one small area on the southern side of the harbour at Lower Town.

The greatest concentrations in Pembrokeshire were at Tenby and Solva, and at the river port of Haverfordwest. But they were also to be found at smaller harbours such as Dale and Porthclais, and on exposed beaches like St. Bride's and Newgale. Almost every creek along the Haven, from Angle to Blackpool, had one or more; even the islands boasted their kilns.

They ranged in size from tiny pot kilns, less than a man's height, to giant draw kilns well over twenty feet tall. A row of the latter (in the 1840s there were no fewer than ten) stood at Prospect Place (Cartlett), Haverfordwest. The remains of the last survivor were recently demolished to make way for a dual carriageway; but their bulk may still be judged by the height of the retaining wall alongside the road.

Nowhere are they more evident than along the Dewisland Peninsula. They are to be seen at virtually every tiny cove where a small vessel might be beached, and where a cart could reach the shore. They stand sentinel, like miniature fortresses, above the tideline; often ivy-covered and crumbling, they serve as a reminder of a bygone age.

II; Friends of Agriculture

Over the centuries Dewisland, in common with much of Pembrokeshire, has been a considerable corn producing area. Much of this was exported by sea, largely to Bristol; a practice which ceased only in the early years of this century. The principal cereal crops were oats and barley, which were better suited to the cool, moist climate of Pembrokeshire. However, some wheat was grown, chiefly in the western peninsulas of Castlemartin and Dewisland, while in early times rye was also of some importance.

In order to ensure consistent high yields, it was necessary for the acid soils to be treated; by Elizabethan times lime was becoming increasingly widely used for this purpose. Limestone was readily available, mostly south of Milford Haven, while a series of coal measures stretched across the county from St. Bride's Bay to Carmarthen Bay.

Although coal and limestone are often found in close proximity, it was not the custom to produce quicklime on the site for transport by ship to the north of the county. The reason is that quicklime reacts with water to form slaked lime, with the evolution of a large amount of heat. Quicklime was therefore an extremely hazardous cargo to transport, and the raw materials were carried by small coastal vessels to various sites around the coast, where the process of lime burning was carried out.

The little ships were usually beached, and their cargoes unloaded into carts which carried them to the limekilns. These were generally sited as near the water's edge as possible.

The kilns were normally built against a bank, which served as a loading platform for charging them; a slope enabled horse-drawn carts to reach this point. Wherever possible, natural features of the ground were utilised. Even in later times, many of the smaller, more remote kilns were little advanced from the early temporary structures, being constructed of roughly laid stones, packed together with earth. Not surprisingly few of these have survived.

Simple Pot Kilns were usually about 6 to 8 feet high and 10 to 12 feet in diameter; a circular pit in the centre was perhaps 6 or 8 feet across at the top, but narrower towards the base. On either side of the kiln was a fireplace-shaped opening, the drawing arch, which connected to the bottom of the pit by a drawhole which allowed air to enter the kiln and through which burnt lime was withdrawn. The lower part of the kiln was filled with small coal or culm, which was ignited by means of firewood. When the culm had caught fire, small pieces of limestone were added from the top. The fire was then allowed to burn out, before the lime was removed from the bottom of the kiln through the draw hole. According to Barbara George, 1 ton of culm was required to produce 2 to 3 tons of lime in a simple, unlined pot kiln.

The so called Draw Kilns were essentially similar in concept, but they were larger and much better constructed. They were often more than 20 feet

2. The last surviving limekiln at Abercastle is typical of the coastal kilns of North Pembrokeshire.

in height, and the crucibles were lined with firebrick to reduce heat losses. Large draw kilns, such as those at Prospect Place in Haverfordwest, could produce between 3 and 4 tons of lime using 1 ton of culm.

Even the later, commercially operated North Pembrokeshire limekilns, which were generally situated at the proper harbours, were dwarfed by these giants. A typical example at Porthclais was about 12 feet high, with a crucible about 10 feet in diameter at the top. They still tended to be built against a slope, but were provided with properly constructed platforms and ramps, supported by masonry walls. Paved areas at the top served for the storage of limestone and culm.

The main advantage in the operation of these kilns was that extra quantities of limestone were added from time to time. The burnt lime was withdrawn from the bottom at intervals, and the kilns could operate on a more or less continuous basis. By arranging the kilns in pairs, as at Porthclais or Lower Fishguard, lime production could continue even when one of the kilns was temporarily extinguished.

Beside the kilns was generally to be found a small, rude shack, the limeburner's hut. In this hovel he lived, or at least rested during his long working day, for the kilns demanded regular attention.

Although the major use of limestone was in agriculture, some was used for other purposes. It is a constituent of mortar; lime, mixed with sand and water forms a paste which sets to a hard cement - the lime slowly absorbing carbon dioxide from the air and changing back to calcium carbonate.

3. The eastern group of draw kilns at Kiln Park, Tenby, with their tall pointed drawing arches.

Another, much smaller, use is very characteristic of the locality. This is the limewash which was once widely applied to the cottage walls. Kilvert, visiting St. David's in 1871, was dazzled by the whitewash on the houses. It was the the custom to add small amounts of 'blue' to the lime to obtain a sparkling finish - an early application of a brightening agent. However, in the rain all the cottages turned to a dull blue-grey colour.

In the past, lime was used for its effect as a disinfectant on the interior walls of kitchens and outbuildings and on the stonework surrounding wells. Not even the cathedral escaped; the walls and pillars of the nave were limed by the Puritans to cover the medieval wall paintings.

But the great bulk of the lime was sold to the farmers, who carried it away to spread on the land. Here the rain slaked it to form an alkali which dissolved and penetrated the ground, where it neutralized the acid soils, thereby increasing the fertility of the land.

Limestone is a fairly hard, naturally occurring form of calcium carbonate. When strongly heated, calcium carbonate decomposes, giving off the gas carbon dioxide, and forming the white, less-hard, solid, calcium oxide or quicklime. One ton of pure calcium carbonate yields a little over half a ton of calcium oxide.

Calcium oxide reacts with water giving off large amounts of heat, forming the grey, paste-like solid called calcium hydroxide or slaked lime. This process is known as slaking of lime. Calcium hydroxide is soluble in water producing a moderately strong alkali. This reacts with any acid which may be present in the soil, enhancing its ability to yield good crops.

Calcium carbonate is itself capable of neutralizing acids, and is a much less unpleasant substance than calcium oxide. Why, therefore, was the expensive and labour intensive process of lime burning adopted?

The reason is that calcium carbonate is insoluble in water (though it dissolves slightly in rain water) and is only effective when finely powdered. Limestone is a relatively hard substance which was difficult to crush to a sufficient extent; only with modern machinery did this become possible. Calcium oxide, on the other hand, crumbles readily, particularly on the addition of water, and is soluble. Consequently the process of lime burning was continued for many centuries.

The principal source of limestone in Pembrokeshire was at West Williamston, near Carew. Small canals were dug to the quarries from the Carew River, enabling coastal sloops and barges to be loaded directly at the quarries. The latter carried the limestone to the kilns at Haverfordwest or elsewhere around the Haven - or to Lawrenny Quay, where it was transhipped into larger craft which transported it around the coast. Elsewhere on the Haven there were limestone quarries on the river below Pembroke and south of Haverfordwest. In the south of the county limestone was exported from Stackpole Quay, from exposed beaches such as Lydstep and from Caldey Island. From these large quantities of limestone were exported to the West Country as well as the west coast of Wales.

Of the Dewisland harbours, only Solva and Porthclais were, from early times, provided with quays; the harbour at Porthgain was first developed in 1851, towards the end of the limestone trade. In North Pembrokeshire only Fishguard (Lower Town) and Newport (Parrog) were similarly provided. Even at these harbours it was the custom to unload the limestone into the harbour at high tide; from there it was taken by cart to the loading platforms of the kilns.

The coal or culm was loaded into ships at quays at Hook and elsewhere along the shores of Milford Haven, or from the beach at Nolton Haven. On Carmarthen Bay the beaches at Amroth and Wiseman's Bridge were used before the construction of the harbour at Saundersfoot in the 1830s. On arrival at their destination the sloops were beached at high tide and the culm loaded directly into carts for transport to the kilns.

The limestone had first to be broken into smaller pieces before it was burned. Then the kiln was filled and the fire lit. The evil-smelling fumes and the dust must have made the task of the limeburner, as he charged the kiln, a particularly unpleasant one even for those days. Then, from time to time, the lime had to be raked out from the kiln. Any speck of lime which touched the burner's skin would immediately be slaked by his sweat, causing painful blisters; to prevent this it was the custom to smear butter or fat over his face and hands.

The coal found in Pembrokeshire is high grade anthracite, which produces

4. The crucibles of two of the Solva Harbour kilns, with the base of the old limeburner's hut.

almost no ash or clinker when it burns, the only residues being agriculturally beneficial. There was, therefore, no necessity to separate these impurities from the lime to be used on the land, a factor which helped to ensure the survival of the simple Pembrokeshire kilns until comparatively recent times.

Living in the neighbourhood of a working limekiln cannot have been a pleasant experience. Fortunately in both Fishguard and Newport the kilns were outside the main built up areas. In Dewisland, it was only at Solva that the kilns were situated in an urban environment, in days long before there was any Clean Air Act in operation. Porthclais, though part of the "City and Suburbs of St. David's", never consisted of more than an inn and a few cottages, and the other coastal villages were small. Haverfordwest was badly affected, even as late as the mid nineteenth century there were around a dozen large kilns at North Street and Cartlett belching out their noxious fumes. At Tenby though most of the kilns were outside the town there were others at the harbour and at quarries near the Salterns.

Some of the limekilns are square in shape, though the great majority of the coastal kilns are round. Apart from the size of the kiln, the most obvious difference is in the size and shape of the kiln eye. In Gower the openings are normally very wide and reach nearly to the top of the kiln, being in the form of a rounded arch. In South Pembrokeshire the arches are often round, though they are somewhat smaller. In contrast, some of the North Cardiganshire kilns have tall but much narrower openings - sometimes, as at Aberystwyth, three in number. Arches are usually of stone, but the kiln at St.

Bride's has brick arches. The kiln at Church Lake, Neyland, is unusual in that it has only a single, rounded arch. At Kiln Park, Tenby, the western group has rounded arches, while the eastern group has pointed openings.

The typical coastal limekiln of North Pembrokeshire is very different; here the kiln eye is not much more than half the height of the kiln, and fairly narrow. The sides are vertical near the base, then they slope inwards until, at the top, the opening is about 2 feet wide. Across this is laid a heavy stone lintel, which gives great strength to the structure.

The limekilns are generally built of the locally available stone; the kilns at Abereiddi are largely of the local black slate; its friable nature has contributed to their decay. Elsewhere, much harder stone was available, so that the kilns are better preserved. The varied hues of brown and grey, sometimes interspersed, in random fashion, with purple and red, make them among the most attractive of our industrial relics.

Even today they are not without their use; some still serve to store the nets and lobster pots of the local fishermen. And the moss covered fireplace shelters many a coastal walker from the sudden Pembrokeshire storm.

5. *The kiln at St Bride's has a rounded arch, a feature of many of the kilns in the south of the county.*

III; An Ancient Industry

The earliest reference to the importation of limestone into Dewisland is to be found in the *Liber Communis*. This is a record of the accounts of St. David's Cathedral for the year 1385, made by Hugh Felton on behalf of Hugh de Pickton, who was at that time Supervisor of the Fabric of the Cathedral.

During the fifth week of the period, a pyckard (a boatload of perhaps 15 tons) of limestones was landed and William Kyley earned 4 shillings for carting them from Porthcleys to the Churchyard; the cargo itself being valued at £1.2s.9d.. Three weeks later, another consignment was landed at Solfach; while, in the tenth week, another load of limestone and 40 bushels of coal, at 2d. per bushel, arrived at Porthcleys and was carted to the Cathedral. The cost of making (burning) this load came to 3s.6d..

The limestone was presumably required for making mortar for the building work then in progress, It would suggest that the primitive kilns of those days were situated in St. David's and not on the coast. The 10 lbs. of lime carried from Haverfordwest at a cost of 3d. was probably of a better quality required for decorative purposes.

The *Black Book of St. David's* provides an even earlier reference to lime burning. The volume is a survey of the lands of the Bishop of St. David's, dating from 1326. It instructs his tenants at Lamphey to perform the task of carrying coal for burning lime when required.

Construction of the first Norman church at St. David's was begun about 1120, so very likely limestone would have been used to produce mortar some 200 years before the *Black Book* was complied. The earliest kilns for producing lime were probably set up near the cathedral and the castles, which were also built around this time. Traces of such a kiln, measuring about 10 feet by 3 feet, have been found during excavations at the Augustinian Priory at Carmarthen. Carbon dating suggests that it was in use around the year 1100. At Cilgerran the base of a limekiln has been discovered inside the castle.

By the fourteenth century there were limekilns in Haverfordwest. The Borough Records (transcribed by B. G. Charles) refer, in 1371, to a "lyme kyll in Schipstrete" - the present Quay Street. About 1240 a Dominican Friary was founded on land lying between Bridge Street and the river; in 1539 the complex included one or more limekilns.

In 1582 the sum of 10d. was paid for the carriage of lime from the kiln of Jane Catharn (who occupied part of the friary land) for the construction of the quay; the cost of one hundred of lime was 5s.0d.. Following the Dissolution of the Monasteries the church and domestic buildings fell into disrepair; by 1739 Browne Willis could write:

"Ye Friary very little or no remains, ye whole site converted to limekilns."

The *Black Book* provides no direct evidence that lime was employed as a fertilizer during the fourteenth century. There are few records of agriculture from those days, so it is uncertain when the practice of liming the soil became widespread.

The earliest contemporary accounts of the use of lime in Pembrokeshire for agricultural purposes date from Elizabethan times. For these we are indebted to the eminent local historian George Owen of Henllys and his *Description of Pembrokeshire*.

According to Owen, the lime used on the land cost 3s.4d. per bushel. The method of liming varied between the north and south of the county. In the drier southern areas lime was spread on the land, with muck being added during the first year; it was his opinion that, without extra moisture, the lime would be too strong. However, in the more mountainous areas, which were colder and wetter than the south, a good crop was obtained without any muck being added.

Owen, writing about 1600, commented that the use of lime had increased greatly during the previous thirty or forty years, so that it had become the chief method of treating the soil. He noted that it destroyed furze, heath and other (acid loving) shrubs, and that it produced sweet, fine grass. He gave his opinion that it had greatly enriched those who made use of it, and quoted an old Pembrokeshire saying:

> "A man doth sand for himself, lime for his son, and marl for his grandchild."

To Owen we also owe the earliest description of a Pembrokeshire limekiln:

> "The limestone being dug in the quarry in great stones, is hewn to the bigness of a man's fist and less to the end that they might the sooner burn through, and being made small the same is put into a kiln made of wall six foot high, four or five foot broad at the rim but growing narrower to the bottom, having two loopholes in the bottom which they call the kiln eyes. In this kiln first is made a fire of coals or rather culm (which is but the dust of coals) which is laid in the bottom of the kiln, and some sticks of wood to kindle the fire. Then is the kiln filled with these small pieces of limestones and then, fire being given, the fire burneth for .... days and maketh the limestones to become mere red fiery coals, which being done and the fire quenched, the lime so burned is suffered to cool in the kiln and then is drawn forth through the kiln eyes, and in this sort is carried to the land where it is laid in heaps. And the next shower of rain maketh it to moulder and fall into dust, which they spread on the land and so sow wheat or barley therein as the time of year requireth."

It was Owen's opinion that the most fertile part of Pembrokeshire was

6. The base of the kiln at Cilgerran Castle, the oldest to date discovered in Pembrokeshire.

Castlemartin, followed by Roose, Narberth and Dewisland. He described Dewisland as being, in parts, very fruitful for corn; complaints that Dewisland barley was 'oaty' he attributed to indifferent husbandry in sowing poor seed. He had not seen better or finer land, or greater store of growing corn, than around St. David's. In previous times it was reported that an acre of land would yield a hundred bushels of barley (a Dewisland bushel was more than double a Winchester bushel) though more recently the harvests had been less good.

In Owen's time, lime was not the only treatment that the Pembrokeshire farmers applied to the land to increase its fertility. In Mid-Pembrokeshire, marl, which is a mixture of limestone and clay, was used to good effect, though it was slow acting; however in Dewisland and north of the Preseli Hills this was not available, Here it was the custom to use sea sand, which was carried from the shore and spread over the land. It was thought, by many, to be superior to lime for the growing of corn, and was to some extent replacing the latter, though its effect was limited to a few years. Sea sand invariably contains a small amount of finely ground calcium carbonate produced from the remains of crushed shellfish; this would help to counteract the acidity of the land. However its longer-term action is probably limited to its effect of lightening the soil.

In the coastal regions it was also the custom to spread seaweed on the land. Some of the kelp was washed up by storms, the rest was cut from the rocks. It was then allowed to rot down, before being spread on the land in the same way as manure; but like manure its effect lasted for only one season.

Apart from the manure which the animals provided, the only indigenous soil conditioners available to the North Pembrokeshire farmer were sea sand and sea ore or seaweed. By Elizabethan times the corn exports were considerable, and the need for lime to treat the soil more effectively had become vital.

Owen provides no information concerning the carriage of limestone by sea, nor do the *Welsh Port Books* normally record voyages between Pembrokeshire ports. However, a few cargoes to outside destinations, such as Cardigan and Wexford, are mentioned during the seventeenth century.

However the *Port Books* show that corn was being exported from North Pembrokeshire. A cargo of pilcorn, wheat and rye was carried in *Marie* of Fishguard from her home port to Barmouth in 1566. In 1577 *Steven* of St. David's carried wheat, malt and peas to Caernarfon, while in 1602 *Guift* of Solva took wheat and barley malt to Wexford. At other times these vessels would presumably have been involved in the local culm and limestone trade.

Some idea of the importance of lime in agriculture during the late sixteenth century is provided for the hundred of Cemais. In 1594, tenants of the Manor of Eglwyswrw had, among other duties, to spend one day with a horse carrying lime from Haverfordwest, a distance of some 20 miles; a day's work was valued at 6d..

7. A simple pot kiln at Abereiddi, similar to those described by George Owen.

It was the custom of the farmers to provide each field with a descriptive name, in North Pembrokeshire these were mostly Welsh. The names are recorded on the various Tithe Maps; it is not unusual for the name *Calch* (lime) to appear. An Estate Map of Trelethin, near St. David's, dated 1762, names two fields north-west of the farmsteads as *Tir Calch* (lime ground), and two others as *Llain Tir Calch* (lime ground strip): all are marked on the map (which shows the intermingled holdings of John Tucker and Thomas Williams) as being arable land. The names were probably old even then, providing evidence of the long history of liming the land in the locality.

Another name which occurs occasionally is *Odyn* (kiln). There is a *Parc yr Odyn* on Porthclais land immediately above the quay; the equivalent *Kiln Park* is common in the south of the county, the best known example being at Tenby.

However '*odyn*', like kiln, is not restricted to limekilns; many farms, like Treginnis Isaf, had a kiln for drying barley for malt. The *Parc yr Odyn* adjoining the farmhouse at Longhouse probably refers to a malting kiln; the field above the limekilns at nearby Abercastle being known as *Parc Penrallt*.

The next detailed survey of agriculture in Pembrokeshire was carried out by Charles Hassall in 1794. It was his contention that the county was not really suited to the growing of corn, although he observed that it was a popular crop. He noted that the chief manure of the district was lime, which was plentiful in the southern part of the county, and was carried by sea around the coast. He observed that, as in Owen's time, sea sand was used widely and successfully on the land in the St. David's area.

A major source of this was Solva Harbour, much being brought ashore at the Sand Quay. In 1791 an Act was made for improving various roads, including that from St. David's to Caerfai; at the same time a track was cut down to the beach to enable sand to be obtained for treating the land.

One handicap to the use of lime was the duty levied on the culm which was required for its production. Hassall commented that if the duty was removed - as it had been in Scotland the previous year - it would be beneficial to agriculture in North Pembrokeshire.

In his view it was necessary to treat an acre of land with about six cartloads of lime in order to produce a good crop of corn. Provided the farmer did not attempt to grow wheat for too long before laying down his land for grass he should then be successful; though few farmers did practice a sensible system of crop rotation.

The recommended local practice for wheat production was to add the lime to fallow land, followed by farmyard muck. For the growing of barley it was customary to mix the lime with road sweepings or ditch earth.

Not all the farmers were convinced of the value of lime; one who questioned its use was John Williams who farmed at Trearched, near Llanrhian, at this time. A diary (transcribed by Francis Green) in which he records his farming operations, gives his views on the subject.

"The old custom was to fallow the ground for wheat; the rotation was wheat, barley, oats, barley, oats and lay ground. I found that by dressing the land well and manuring, the crops were not much. What I thought first was to manure the land with lime. About the 26th year of my age (1796) I began to consider what effect it had. All my neighbours used it as manure but could not say which way it affected the soil. It is certain found to kill chickweed and some other weeds. The query is whether anything can kill weeds and nourish grass as they are so near in nature. Lime certainly does not show itself the first year as dung and compost does."

He also carried on a correspondence with Peter Williams, his uncle, who was a merchant in Bristol. Among other subjects, the letters deal with the rising cost of wheat and other cereals, which more than doubled in the three years from December 1797; there is also mention of the trade in corn and butter from Abercastle to Bristol.

The log book of Abel Hicks of Trecadwgan gives some idea of the extent of the corn trade in the 1760s. In 1761, in the *Industrious Bee,* he made two voyages from Haverfordwest to Belfast with wheat and malt and one to Dublin with barley and malt. During the following year he sailed three times to Liverpool and twice to Belfast, carrying mainly wheat, and once (in October) to Liverpool with oats. The 1762 harvest must have been a poor one as in 1763 there were only single cargoes of oats for Northam (Devon) and Liverpool.

During the eighteenth century, limestone was imported into Porthclais for building purposes as well as for agricultural use. In 1743 a cargo of nine tons of limestone arrived, together with the culm to burn it. Evidence that there were already limekilns at Porthclais is provided by the fact that, during the same year, eleven loads of lime were carted to the cathedral at a cost of 9d. per load. The material was required for the reconstruction of the Chapter House which was then taking place.

There are no detailed maps of Solva or Porthclais for this period, so it is difficult to draw conclusions as to the number and size of the kilns in use at that time. However, the cathedral authorities spent a considerable amount of money on repairing the pier wall at Porthclais in 1722 in order to improve the harbour, while Solva started to prosper about 1756.

The limekilns would probably have been improved at the same time, and some of the larger limekilns probably date from the middle of the century. There were kilns on the east side of the harbour at Abercastle, which were owned by the Vaughan family; a lease of 1774 refers to a house being built on waste land between the mill and the limekilns.

The Vaughans also owned the Fishguard kilns at this time. The Court Rolls of the Manor of Newport for 1751 mention four kilns within the town. Two were in Bridge Street; one had been built by James Bowen and Thomas Knolles, the other by Owen Lewis. Another, at the lower end of St. Mary Street, had been built by William Warren; the fourth was in High Street. All were on waste land belonging to the lord of the manor. It would seem that by the middle of the eighteenth century the lime industry of North Pembrokeshire was already well developed.

Haverfordwest

IV; The Years of Prosperity

The end of the eighteenth century and the beginning of the nineteenth was a period of prosperity as far as the agriculture of Pembrokeshire was concerned. Evidence of this is to be seen in the large number of substantial farmhouses which were built or extended during this time.

One of the reasons for this was the war with France, which had cut off some of the normal sources of supply of wheat and other corn. Dewisland and much of South Pembrokeshire had long been famed for growing cereals, and the farmers were not slow to take advantage of the opportunity presented to them.

Increased corn production meant an increase in the demand for lime to treat the land. In turn this led to a a need for extra limestone to be imported, together with the culm to burn it. Solva - by far the largest of the Dewisland harbours, being capable of handling vessels of 500 tons and upwards - was particularly well situated to cope with the demand. A shipping company was formed in 1756, after which the port developed rapidly. By about 1800 there were some 30 vessels belonging to Solva, mainly small craft of between 20 and 40 tons, but including brigs of up to 250 tons.

The principal exports from Solva were corn and butter, while the main imports were coal and limestone. Most of the trade was coastwise, but there was some with Ireland and even with America. Eventually extensive quays were constructed along the western side of the harbour, including Trinity Quay, which was developed in connection with the construction of the second Smalls Lighthouse in 1856.

Porthclais was a much smaller harbour, being limited to ships of about 100 tons. It also traded regularly with Bristol, exporting corn and butter and importing general merchandise; as in Solva, the granaries in the lower part of St. David's serve as a reminder of the times. There were also considerable imports of coal and limestone from South Pembrokeshire. Only half a dozen boats were based here, and they were small, averaging only 25 tons. But they were ideal for the coal and limestone trade, and for carrying corn to Bristol. In spite of its limited size, Porthclais, with its protective breakwater, was a snug refuge for shipping.

Although it never possessed any proper quays, north-facing Abercastle provided a sheltered anchorage. Several vessels were operated from Abercastle, the largest being of about 100 tons. It carried on a similar trade to its neighbours, and was of particular significance, as it was the harbour which served the rich corn growing area around Mathry - the Golden Prebend.

Porthgain, in its present form, is a commercial port of the early twentieth century, exporting slate, bricks and granite on a large scale. Until about 1850, when the original harbour was built, it consisted of nothing more than a couple of cottages and the limeklins at the head of a creek.

8. The pair of kilns on the eastern quay at Porthclais, showing the interior of the damaged square kiln.

The remaining kilns were situated on what were virtually open beaches where the broad-beamed smacks could be run aground. During the nineteenth century some slate was exported from Abereiddi, but otherwise these landing places had no real trade, except culm and limestone for the kilns and the occasional cargo of contraband.

However they possessed the advantage of providing cheap and convenient transport to the more remote areas. At best they had a sandy bottom on which the vessels were beached while their cargoes were unloaded. Owing to the exposed nature of the landing beaches the trade was limited to the summer months; the unprotected bays, with their dangerous surrounding reefs, were no place to be caught in adverse weather. During the winter months, those ships not engaged in the corn trade could lie up in one of the better protected havens.

The largest and most important harbour on the north coast of Pembrokeshire was Fishguard. At the beginning of the nineteenth century some 50 ships belonged to the port. About half of these were sloops of up to 50 tons engaged in carrying culm and limestone and in trade with Bristol; the rest were larger brigs and schooners which, for the most part, did not trade locally. Trade with Bristol involved the export of considerable quantities of corn (chiefly oats) and butter in return for general shop goods; other imports included coal and timber. The trade was centred on the old harbour at Lower Town, though culm and limestone were also landed on the beach at Goodwick.

9. The restored round kiln on the quay at Parrog, Newport, with its adjacent limeburner's cottage.

Newport, though smaller than Fishguard, was essentially similar in its commerce; among the vessels owned at the port were many sloops which were involved in its culm and limestone trade. Otherwise there were no harbours along the rocky coast between Fishguard and Cardigan, only unprotected beaches like Pwllgwaelod and Ceibwr; here ships would, in fair weather, come in on one tide, unload, and be ready to sail on the next. The narrow, tortuous lane which leads to Ceibwr perhaps explains why coastal ketches sailed here with coal even after the First World War; once most of the coastal villages were as isolated.

To these and to scores of other landing places around the coast and the shores of Milford Haven, came, during the summer months, an endless stream of sloops loaded with culm and limestone. At the larger harbours there might be a queue of ships waiting to unload; the more remote creeks might see only one or two ships in the whole season.

Most of the Pembrokeshire harbours were involved in the export of corn. The Bills of Entry for the Port of Bristol for 1835 record 41 corn shipments from Haverfordwest, 3 from Tenby, 4 from Pembroke and 23 from Milford.

Massive granaries were erected, during the late eighteenth and early nineteenth centuries, on and near the quays to store the grain until the winter months when it would command the highest prices in the English markets. Stoutly built, usually between three and five storeys high - the corn was stored on the upper floors - they towered above the surrounding buildings.

At one time warehouses lined almost the entire length of Haverfordwest quay below New Bridge. Several have since been demolished, but others survive, mainly around the Bristol Trader, including what is probably the largest and finest example in the county. Already some two centuries old, they will probably long outlast the nearby twentieth century commercial developments. Elsewhere fine examples are to be seen on the quays at Tenby and Lower Town, Fishguard, and in Main Street, Solva; there are smaller warehouses on the quay in Pembroke and at the Parrog, Newport, while at lonely Abercastle the harbour is overlooked by the gaunt remains of an old granary.

In the early nineteenth century the limestone trade was handled mainly by single-masted, fore-and-aft rigged vessels known as smacks and sloops; their crews normally consisted of three men - master, mate and a seaman who was often a mere boy. Only later were these joined by two-masted ketches, also fore-and-aft rigged, which were more manoeuvrable than the single-masted boats, an important consideration when sailing in restricted channels.

It was normal for ownership of these craft to be shared among several persons. The St. David's smack *Favourite Nancy* of 17 tons was owned by George Perkins, farmer, (16 shares); John Rees, mariner, (16); George Williams, merchant, (16); his brother John Williams, farmer, (8); and William Davies, farmer, (8). All would have had an interest in the culm and limestone trade.

According to Samuel Lewis, these ships spent the summer months carrying limestone, coal and culm from the south of the county, while during the winter they took out corn (chiefly barley) and butter to Bristol and other English towns.

One of the craft engaged in the trade during the first half of the nineteenth century was the Abercastle sloop *Ranger*; registered at 25 tons she carried about 40 tons of cargo. Included in her cargoes were were limestone from the Pembroke area and culm from Little Milford (near Hook) for both Abercastle and Porthgain; in 1839 she carried 10 cargoes of limestone from Lawrenny to Abercastle. Other destinations included Fishguard and Dinas. In 1864 *Kitty*, whose cargo capacity was about 24 tons, brought 11 loads of limestone and 13 of culm from Milford River to St. David's; she also made 2 voyages to Bristol. Around mid-century perhaps a score of ships were involved with the limestone trade of Dewisland.

The Pembrokeshire coast was a dangerous one in the days of sail, and the small ships engaged in the local trade were not immune. Samuel Williams, who was a Lloyd's Agent, listed the ships wrecked or disabled around St. David's between 1825 and 1870: among the local casualties he named *Pilgrim* of Solva, *Brothers* of Milford and *Eliza* of St. David's, all carrying limestone. Vessels lost while carrying culm included *Rechabite* of Fishguard, *Alligator* of Solva and *Mary* of St. David's. The names of most of these are to be found among the Bristol records of trade.

10. 'The Curious Little Creek of Solva ...', from a watercolour by John 'Warwick' Smith, dated 1795.

Towards the end of the eighteenth century it became the fashion among artists to visit St. David's to draw the cathedral and its surroundings. They passed through Solva, and many of them sketched the harbour. From this chance the development of Solva is well documented.

One of the earliest illustrations of Solva is a watercolour by John 'Warwick' Smith, which is dated 1795. The view from near Harbour House shows clearly three of the quartet of kilns which now stand at the water's edge below the Gribin. On the bank behind the kilns is the limeburner's hut; while just beyond the group is a small quay, which is marked on the plan of Solva Harbour drawn in 1748 by Lewis Morris.

The scene shows several sloops and small square-rigged vessels; a horse-drawn cart makes its way towards the kilns and a laden packhorse carries lime away. There do not seem to be any proper quays on the opposite side of the harbour; there are few houses in Upper Solva, while the two halves of the village are linked by a narrow track where the main road now runs.

Others came later; their drawings show something of the kilns, often with a pall of smoke hanging over them. They show, too, the rapid growth of the settlement, and the improvements being made to the landing stages during the early nineteenth century.

At the beginning of the century, Richard Fenton, who was a native of St. David's, made an extensive tour of the county. He came to Solva, and he saw the limekilns:

Solva

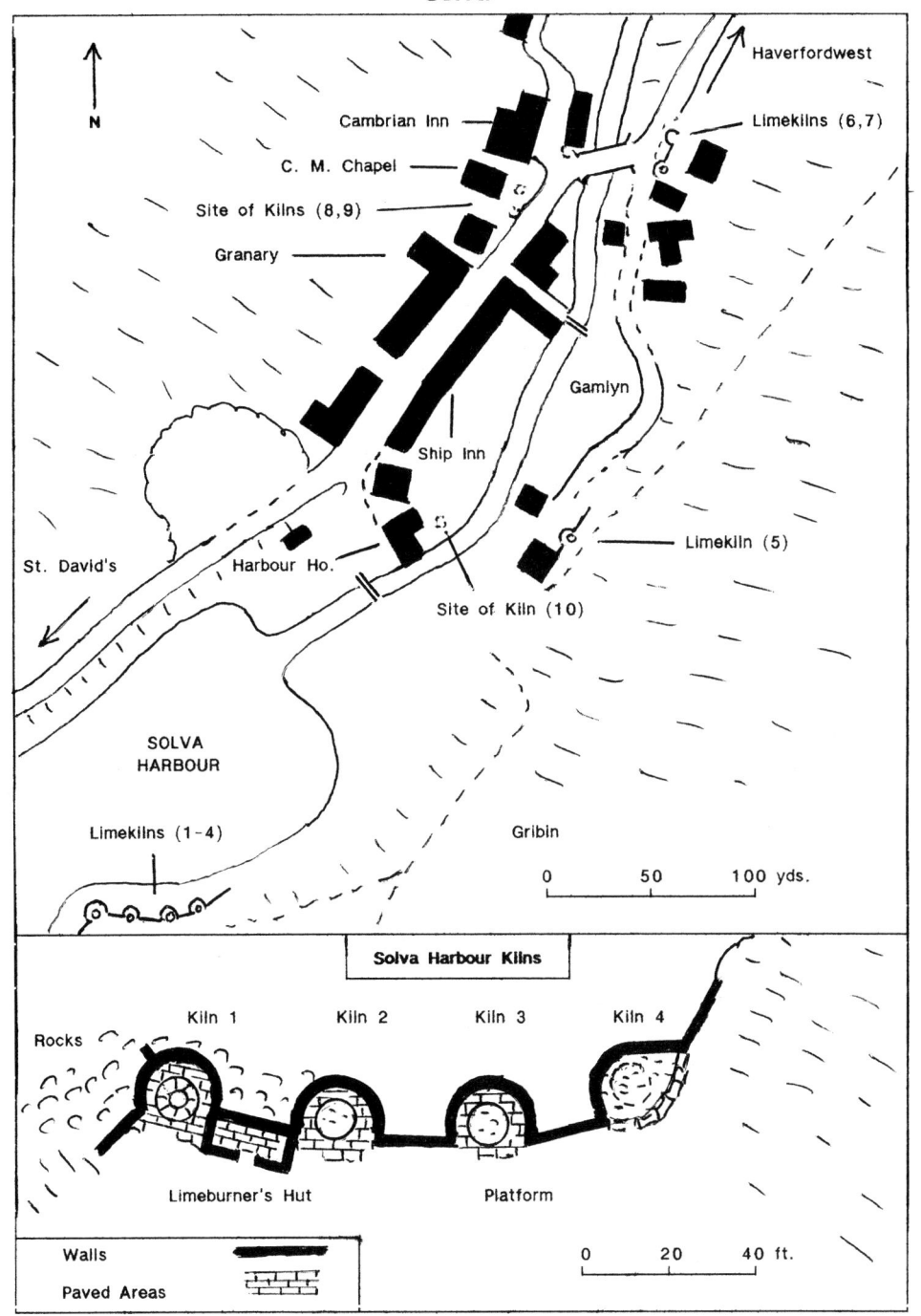

"Solva may be divided into an upper town and a lower town ..... The lower town, affecting to get into the form of a street, would not be very unpleasant or very irregular were it not for two lime kilns placed in the centre of the western row and rather too far forward in it, whose hot vapour and the dust and noise incident to them, make them very offensive, proving a great drawback on a residence of that part of the town where the chief shops and warehouses are and the trade of the place is carried on; yet these friends of agriculture, though in this case nuisances, from having existed prior to the thought of any houses will be able to maintain their ground and it would be difficult perhaps to prevail on their owners to destroy them."

Their exact position is shown on a plan of Lower Solva dated 1839. It shows them standing almost opposite Solva Bridge, on ground later to be occupied by the forecourt of the Calvinistic Methodist Chapel, and well in front of the line of the Cambrian Inn which adjoins it. Also shown are the four waterside kilns and the one behind Harbour House. In an enclosed and sheltered valley, Lower Solva must have been a far from pleasant place to reside.

Another area visited by early nineteenth century artists was Fishguard. One view of the town and harbour from the north - by an unknown artist -

11. 'The Lower Town and Harbour of Fishguard', from a drawing c. 1800 by Sir Richard Colt Hoare.

shows there were in 1806 kilns on six sites in and around the Slade; most, if not all, appear to have been single kilns. About the same time, Sir Richard Colt Hoare made a drawing of Lower Town showing the houses and quays with a couple of small sloops in the harbour. In the foreground are two of the kilns, one above the other, on the western side of the Slade. The design of these seems very similar to that of the surviving pair. A third contemporary drawing by Henry Gastineau shows that at least one pair of kilns existed at the Slade.

By the nineteenth century, the burning of limestone was being carried out on a commercial scale, and the occupation of lime burner was an important one. Pigot's *Commercial Directory of South Wales* for 1836 lists John Howell, Michael James and Thomas John at Solva and George Williams at St. David's; in this context the lime burner was the proprietor of the kilns. They were men of some substance; at Solva, James Howell occupied the Cambrian Inn and was a corn merchant and shopkeeper, while Thomas John was also a shopkeeper, and Michael James a corn merchant and tallow chandler. At St. David's, George Williams was in addition a corn merchant and miller.

The lime burners did not necessarily own the kilns. At Porthclais in 1840 there were two limekilns on each of Porthclais Farm and Upper Porthllisky, and one on Rhoscribed. The harbour kilns at Solva were on land owned by the Lort Phillips family and were occupied by Michael James. By this time, at St. David's, Samuel Williams, merchant and shipowner, had succeeded his father as lime burner

Not all the kilns were the property of wealthy landlords; some were owned by groups of farmers. James Harries, gentleman, of Trenichol, who died in 1829, left to his widow a one-sixth share in a limekiln at Solva, and also shares in the Milford-registered sloop *Mary*. The businessmen of nineteenth century Dewisland were indeed men of many parts.

In 1870 all the remaining Porthclais kilns were the property of Charles Allen; two being occupied by Thomas Davies and two by William Williams. The latter, who lived at Grove Hotel, was a landlord and corn and coal merchant, as well as a shipowner. His *Two Brothers*, and *Jane, William* and *True Bess*, owned respectively by Michael James, John Howell and Samuel Williams, were just some of the small craft which belonged to the local lime burners. By 1840, single ownership of vessels was becoming fairly common.

By 1880, only John Williams, corn, seed and coal merchant, remained as lime burner in Solva; twenty years earlier there had been Stephen Lewis and John Owen as well. The days of the lime burners were coming towards their end. John Williams, Ship Inn, who had taken over from his father-in-law Michael James, was the last of the major shipowner merchants of Solva; though his son, Samson Thomas Williams, kept one kiln alight until the end of the century.

In Haverfordwest the Bridge Street kilns had been demolished by the beginning of the nineteenth century and the Black Horse erected on the site; the Quay Street kilns (which were apparently located near the New Quay) had also presumably vanished. Lime burning had become centred at North Gate and particularly across the river at Cartlett. There were other individual kilns in existence during the nineteenth century at the Marsh and in Prendergast near the junction of the Fishguard and Cardigan roads.

During the 1830s the North Gate kilns were operated by Thomas Evans, while at Cartlett (where a sale map of 1840 shows no fewer than 10 kilns in existence) there were four limeburners, each operating one or more kilns - William John of Prendergast, Thomas Llewhellin of Quay Street, Thomas Maddocks of Bridge Street and James Rogers of Cartlett. By 1858 George Ormond had taken over at North Gate, while at Cartlett the old established John and Rogers families had been joined by Stephen Jenkins of Prendergast and Robert Wrench of Cambrian Place.

The 25" Ordnance Survey Map of 1888 shows four kilns at North Gate and seven at Cartlett; and they were large. Haverfordwest was centrally placed for the distribution by horse and cart of lime to a large area of Mid-Pembrokeshire. Before the building of the New Bridge, sloops could discharge their cargoes of culm and limestone in the basin which existed just across the road from the Cartlett kilns. Afterwards barges could still reach the basin, where the Riverside development now stands, though larger sailing ships had to unload below New Bridge.

Only Stephen Jenkins and Thomas John were mentioned in Slater's 1880 edition of the *Directory of South Wales*. As elsewhere the demand for lime was diminishing rapidly. A sale notice of 1856 refers to a ruined limekiln at the upper end of Prendergast. By the end of the century the site of the North Gate kilns had been built over; now only the name Kiln Road serves to recall them.

In the latter part of the nineteenth century, there were limekilns in Goodwick as well as at Lower Town in Fishguard. Of the Goodwick kilns, one was on the shore near the western end of the beach, a second at the bottom of Goodwick Hill and two others at Dyffryn. The latter was the home of Thomas Lewis, owner of the sloop *Britannia*, and one of two men listed in 1870 as limeburners in Fishguard and Goodwick. The other, David Williams of Drim, also lived in Goodwick and was the owner of the sloop *Anne & Mary*. Perhaps the fact that the Fishguard Harbour Improvement Company at that time imposed a toll of 1d. per registered ton on the importation of culm and limestone, while Goodwick beach was free of such charges, contributed to the success of the Goodwick burners.

The method of applying lime to the land, as practised in North Pembrokeshire, was costly in terms of time and labour. Francis Green, writing around 1920, describes the methods used, as related to him by some of the old farmers.

Liming was usually carried out on newly ploughed fields. The soil was removed from strips, each two furrows wide, at regular intervals across the

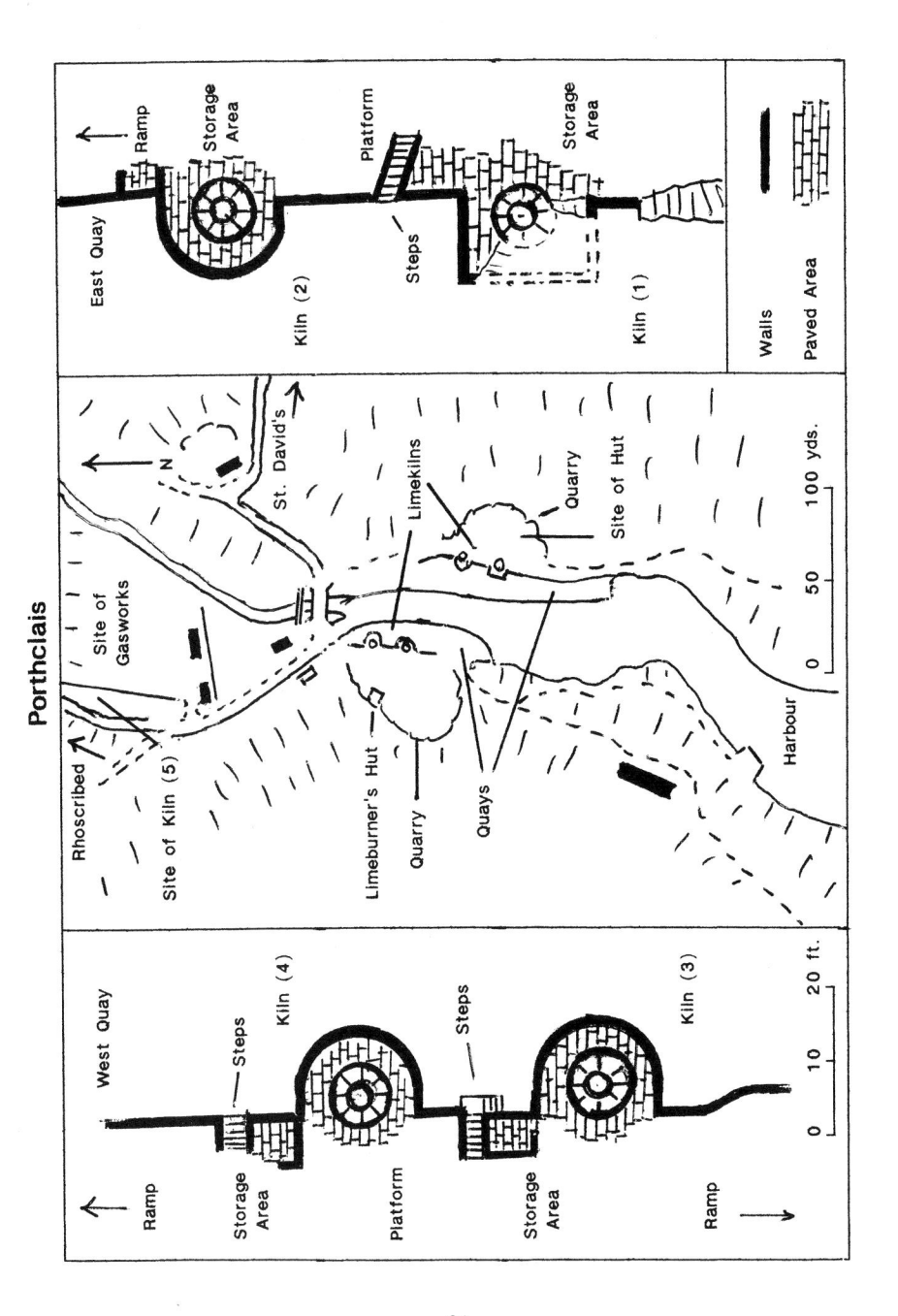

Porthclais

field, and carried to the side of the hedge. Lime was brought from the kiln and mixed with this earth; the pile was then turned over to ensure that earth and lime were well mixed. Finally the soil was carted back and spread over the field.

The more prosperous farmers would often purchase several boatloads of limestone, though several small farmers might share a single cargo. The process was only economic as long as wages were low, and reached its peak in the early years of the nineteenth century.

An account of the operation of the limekilns at Porthclais at the end of the nineteenth century, shortly before they closed, is given by John Miles Thomas in *Looking Back*, which is a fascinating account of his boyhood in St. David's around the turn of the century:

"We boys from Lower Moor spent endless time around Porthclais, which was then busy with trade in coal and culm principally, and also at times, limestone, which was burnt in the kilns, of which there were at least four in general use. The coal and culm was off loaded onto carts which would come alongside the little ships when the tide was out, that is for about six hours each tide.

A favourite pastime at Porthclais was to watch the limeburner John y Galchen, a pale man who took charge of the lime-kilns. Ships brought the limestone and threw it overboard at a place above and to the left of the bend in the harbour. This was done at high tide so that it was well up the mouth of the harbour. John y Galchen spent some time breaking up the limestone into small pieces before lighting the kiln. When he was ready, he gathered a great heap of firewood and anything that would burn to start the fire, then a layer of small anthracite on top of the firewood. When the coal burned, he would put on a layer of limestone, and so continue with layers of coal and limestone until the kiln was full to the top when it would burn with a blue flame. On the leeward side it discharged an unpleasant smell of unburnt gases, so we stood on the windward side and tried to warm ourselves and watched the little blue flames dancing about on the surface of the fire. After a few days the bottom of the kiln was opened and the lime withdrawn. Carts would then take the lime to the farmer's fields. The kiln was recharged twice a day and would keep on burning for weeks at a time."

It was not only schoolboys who enjoyed the warmth which the limekilns provided. They were used as meeting places by the young men of the locality who sometimes, when they had imbibed too freely, would spend the night cosseted by their warmth rather than return home.

Some of those who gathered at the kilns were undesirable characters. On 16th June, 1841, John Tamlyn of Victoria Place, Haverfordwest, published a notice addressed to the Mayor and other authorities of the Town and County of Haverfordwest.

12. Porthclais as John Miles Thomas would have known it at the turn of the century.

"I have to complain of a public nuisance. The Lime-kilns at the North Gate, appear to me to be a complete nursery for blackguards, inasmuch as they sit around the top of the Lime-kilns, in the winter nights in particular, and put their heads together, and consult about committing a robbery on the Poultry houses of every kind of Feathered Fowls. I am sorry to say that I have been repeatedly robbed in this way; and I am told, that they plaister them with clay, and then roast them on the Lime-kilns in the night; and thereby enjoy a feast at my expense.

The late Mr. Charles Hassall (who lodged at the house of Mr. Gibbs, the Saddler, in former days, long before I came into this country), said to me, that Haverfordwest was always considered to be a very immoral town. However, let it be as it may, I was last night pursued through the fields by a riotous set of boys, at the North Gate; and if they cannot conduct themselves better, they most certainly ought to be transported.

I do not wish to cast any severe reflections without a sufficient cause; yet, owing to the conduct of these young blackguards, I take a roundabout way, and come in and out of Haverfordwest by the City Road.

I hope that in future I shall not have any reason to complain of insults, that I never experienced in any other town during my travels for the last 40 years, through different parts of England and Wales."

Cartlett Lime Kilns,
Haverfordwest,
1st April 1930

M*essrs* *Davies & Son. Builder & Undertakers*
Co R. G. WARLOW, *Blaencilgoed*
LIME MERCHANT, *Tanllwyth*

Lime delivered to any part in large or small quantities.

Analyst's Report: EXCELLENT QUALITY

1927

13th June	1	Ton ¾ Cwts of Lime dyd to Narberth	1	16	0

Tramps, too, gathered around the kilns on winter nights; but they could be dangerous places for the unwary. There are accounts of men, befuddled by alcohol and by the poisonous fumes exuded by the Cartlett kilns in Haverfordwest, being taken to the local hospital for treatment to their burns. Others, less fortunate, fell victim to the deadly carbon monoxide, not understanding that the blue coloured flame betrayed the presence of this silent killer.

Local newspapers record several such tragedies. One evening in April 1844 an unknown vagrant had been seen passing through Solva village. The following morning his remains had been recovered from one of the local kilns; his sole possessions were a halfpenny, a little tobacco and some bread and cheese. On 28th November, 1862, the terribly burnt body of a young man called George Williams, a native of Spittal, had been recovered from the limekiln in Victoria Road in Milford. There were other hazards. In the early hours of a Sunday in April 1878, a certain Arthur Rees had been seen in an intoxicated state near the Cartlett kilns. He was warned of the danger, but some hours later his body was found where he had fallen inside one of the empty kilns. Less serious was an accident in June 1855 at Wilson's kiln near Haverfordwest Station involving a runaway tram which careered from the top of the kiln to the landing slip.

Although not a primary product of the decomposition of limestone, carbon monoxide was invariably present in the waste gases from both pot and draw kilns. Some of the carbon dioxide formed during the process reacted with the carbon of the coal (Pembrokeshire anthracite is almost pure carbon) to give carbon monoxide. If the air supply was limited, carbon monoxide was also formed by incomplete combustion of the coal.

The limeburner had to judge and adjust the flow of air through the kiln carefully, for if too much air was admitted the temperature of the kiln (normally nearly 1000° C) would rise still further, burning up more coal, to the benefit of the bystanders alone. No matter how skilled the limeburner, he could not really compete with the modern process which uses industrial gas to heat the limestone in enclosed rotary kilns

The scene described by John Miles Thomas was little different from that witnessed by George Owen three hundred years previously. But his generation was destined to be the last to smell the sulphurous fumes of the kilns; soon the little blue flames would dance no more.

13. The Cartlett limekilns, Haverfordwest, serve as a grandstand for spectators of a religious procession in the early twentieth century.

V; The Silent Sentinels

During the second half of the nineteenth century there was a sudden fall in the amount of limestone being burned, so that many of the limekilns went out of production. This is underlined by the 25 inch Ordnance Survey map of 1887, which shows that of the eight surviving limekilns in Solva only one was in production; one of the pair at the foot of Solva Hill. The four Porthclais kilns were still in operation, though these too had closed by 1906, leaving the Solva kiln as the only one working locally.

The causes for the decay of the industry were several. There was a general decline in agriculture due to the availability of cheap imported foodstuffs following the repeal of the Corn Laws. This meant that the growing of corn, in an area of only marginal suitability, was no longer profitable.

The North Pembrokeshire limekilns were small, and just as they had replaced the simple pot kilns of earlier days they were in turn succeeded by larger and more efficient kilns situated nearer the sources of the raw materials. The problems of carrying ready burnt lime were no longer insuperable.

The coming of the railways meant that bulk cargoes could be moved by land much more rapidly and economically than by sea. Railways and the improved roads allowed direct access to the rest of the country for the first time.

The sea, for centuries the lifeline of the area, was no longer the link with the rest of the country. The small, cumbersome smacks and ketches could not compete with the revolution in transport which steam had produced. Some of the ships did fight back by fitting auxiliary engines, but they fought a losing battle. They lingered for a while bringing in coal from South Wales for the coastal communities and carrying stone from Porthgain, but the closing of the quarries at the latter place in 1931 effectively brought coastal trading to an end.

As late as the 1920s there were still ten barges, most of which carried about 15 tons of culm or limestone, trading within the Haven. The tide-assisted voyage from West Williamston to Haverfordwest took about two hours, and a craft like the *Jane*, which carried 30 tons, could make half a dozen round trips per week.

A few large limekilns did last well into the twentieth century. One of the draw kilns at Prospect Place in Haverfordwest, by then owned by R. G. Warlow - in 1902 he purchased the smack *Water Lily* - continued working until the late 1930s, and carts made the laborious journey there to obtain lime. One or two kilns situated, like that at Ludchurch, on the limestone belt survived even longer, but in the end they too succumbed to progress.

By then the demand for lime was small, and could be satisfied from other sources. The advance of modern technology had created machinery capable of producing crushed limestone, which could be used directly on the land.

Ships were bringing cargoes of nitrates from South America, and other new and more effective fertilizers spelled the end of an industry which had continued almost unchanged for at least five hundred years.

Addressing Pembrokeshire farmers in 1866, a Mr. Roach advised against excessive use of lime on the land, which, he said, led to soil exhaustion. Used in moderation it was beneficial, but at a cost of between £3 and £4 per acre he considered it to be less economic than artificial fertilizers.

During the First World War, a Government commissioner was sent to Pembrokeshire to study the feasibility of reopening some of the kilns, but no action was taken. A soil analyst reported that there was a lime deficiency of between 25 cwts. and 5 tons of ground limestone per acre in the county; he also reckoned there was an annual loss of up to 1/2 ton per acre due to drainage.

As late as 1930, the Pembrokeshire County Council was considering the possibility of reviving the procedure of liming the land, and of reopening some of the limekilns. Some farmers did still use lime, but it was largely obtained from Carmarthenshire, where production costs were lower. The aim was twofold; first to revitalise the land, second to deal with the serious unemployment which then existed in the county.

One of those who argued strongly against the scheme was the member for St. David's, Adrian Owen Williams. The process was, he said, too expensive and laborious; no man could be expected to carry out the unpleasant task of lime burning for a wage which the farmers would be prepared to pay.

He spoke from experience: he had, as he said, been one of the last lime burners in the county; at one time he had burned about 400 tons annually. He was the fourth generation of his family to practice the trade; the great grandson of George Williams, who had burned lime a century earlier. Cllr. Williams had operated a coal merchant's business near Solva Bridge, alongside the kilns. In 1907 he had leased from Samson Thomas Williams a number of premises including 'the limekiln near the Gamblin' for a period of seven years.

There was to be no revival of the lime industry in Pembrokeshire. The coastal limekilns had been long disused, and within a few years the remaining kilns operating elsewhere ceased work.

A century has elapsed since the fires in most of the kilns were allowed to go out for the last time. Since then there have been many changes, and the harbours and creeks, once busy with small ships arriving with coal and limestone and loading with corn, nowadays echo to the laughter of visitors.

The shores of Milford Haven are littered with the remains of limekilns; at the beginning of the century there were well over fifty. A few, like that at Landshipping Quay, are well preserved, others lie hidden in the undergrowth. Among the more accessible of the survivors is a somewhat overgrown pair beside the main road at Pickleridge, Dale. South of the village in the wooded valley of Castlebeach are the remains of another kiln and the hut once occupied by the limeburner.

14. The limekiln at Sandy Haven still retains its companion weighbridge.

Around the Haven, as on the limestone belt, the kilns were often built singly, presumably to serve a particular farm. In 1906, dotted along the banks of Sandy Haven, there were 6 kilns; at the time of the Tithe Map, 1840, there had been several others. Two survive in good condition; one on private ground near Sandy Haven Chapel, the other near Sandy Haven Farm. The latter is unique in that the restored complex includes a weighbridge as well as the limeburner's hut and the kiln.

In the towns few kilns survive, though there is one in good condition beneath the town wall in Pembroke at the east end of the Common. The large kiln at Victoria Road in Milford, scene of at least one fatality, has long been demolished and replaced by dockyard buildings. Individual kilns however survive near Black Bridge on Castle Pill and near the head of Priory Pill which, before the construction of Milford Docks, was navigable to this point.

On the Castlemartin Peninsula most of the kilns were built on the limestone belt - in any case there were few suitable landing places. Apart from the Kiln Park complex near Tenby, there is a fine example of a large, square kiln above Stackpole Quay, and there is a more typical round kiln at West Angle. All these were, however, built near limestone quarries.

Many of the Dewisland limekilns have vanished, as have others throughout West Wales. The ever encroaching sea has claimed a few, including at least one of the Abercastle kilns, and possibly the fifth kiln which, according to Warburton, once existed by the water's edge at Solva. The square limekiln at Porthclais - the one nearest the sea - suffered damage when the quay wall was breached; happily both quay and kiln have been restored.

Some have had to make way for progress. The two kilns in the main street of Lower Solva, which had proved so offensive to Fenton, were demolished to make way for the Methodist Chapel; more recently the kiln behind Harbour House was also pulled down. Altogether six kilns survive in Solva out of about twice that number; but, in this respect, Solva is luckier than Haverfordwest where not one still stands. Those who lived in the shadows of the kilns in Quay Street and Bridge Street, in North Street and Cartlett would however hardly have mourned their passing.

While the sturdy larger kilns have survived unless struck by some catastrophe, the small pot kilns of the remote creeks have been less fortunate. Of the two on Poyntz Castle land at Porth Mynawyd only the bank and a few stones remain. Their neighbour on Lochfaen land, in this remote and deserted valley, is overgrown, as is the ruined kiln at Gwadn at the entrance to Solva Harbour. At Abereiddi two fairly small kilns survive, though they are overgrown and partly collapsed. Further east the kiln by the roadside at Aberfelin has vanished completely.

Once there must have been many others of which all records have been

15. The massive square draw kiln at Stackpole Quay.

lost. The earliest kilns were built to last only one season; even those of Owen's day have probably long since disappeared. Many were pulled down and rebuilt, or, after their useful life, dismantled for building stone, as happened to the kiln on Ramsey Island.

Luckily there are several kilns which survive in good condition. The remaining kiln at Abercastle still stands erect, though perilously close to the sea; it could easily succumb, like its former neighbour. They stood on land which once belonged to the bishop and are shown on the plan of Long House contained in his map book of 1815. On the slope above the kiln are the ivy-clad ruins of the limeburner's hut - one of the few of which any trace remains.

Of the eastern kilns (according to R. Moore-Colyer there were three) owned in the last century by the Yorkes of Langton, nothing remains. In 1887 one still stood below the cottages, near the high tide line, but it probably fell victim to the tides soon afterwards. The gaunt ruins of the granary and the solitary limckiln are the only reminders that this was once a busy little port, and home to Captain George of the s.s. *Ben Rein*, one of the last of the coastal traders.

The harbour village of Porthgain is dominated by the enormous ruins of the quarries and brickworks, which tower over the limekilns which were its first industry. One kiln, surprisingly large, stands near the harbour; the square, second kiln is some distance from the sea, halfway up the old track which led past Ynys Fain to Pentop and the quarries. Slate, brick and granite, together lasted some eighty years; the almost forgotten limestone trade spanned several centuries.

The secluded beach of Aberbach is the site of the two surviving limekilns on the rocky peninsula of Pencaer. In 1887 there were four limekilns at Goodwick, which were demolished when the new Fishguard Harbour was built, and there was one at the remote cove of Porthsychan, about a mile east of Strumble Head. Isolated from the rest of Dewisland by a range of miniature mountains, Pencaer has always looked towards the town of Fishguard in neighbouring Cemais rather than to St. David's away to the west.

Unlike the Goodwick kilns, three of the Fishguard kilns have survived, though all are in need of attention. An imposing pair of round kilns stands near the foot of the Slade; the contours of the land mean they are of unequal size, the lower one being unusually large for the north of the county. There is another large kiln on the Musland, east of the bridge, which is completely overgrown; a fourth kiln, visible in early photographs, which stood to the west of the granary has been demolished.

At Newport, an oddly-shaped pair of kilns survives on the quay at Parrog; one of them (a fairly large round kiln) has been restored, along with the adjoining limeburner's cottage, by the National Park Authority. There is nothing remarkable about the kilns themselves, but few of the huts have survived, and none of the others is complete. On the opposite side of the

16. The large limekiln on the north side of the Nevern estuary, with its tall pointed arch; an unusual feature in Pembrokeshire kilns.

estuary, some distance west of the bridge, a much larger and more impressive round kiln has also been renovated; its tall pointed arch is more typical of Cardiganshire kilns. Less happily, two single kilns which once stood near the old warehouse on the Parrog have been destroyed in recent years.

Solva is still the place where the greatest number of kilns can be found. The group of four on the eastern shore of the harbour is one of the most conspicuous features of the village. Built in a row, they do not seem to conform to any set pattern. Possibly they were erected at different times, replacing earlier examples. Standing literally on the shore, only a short distance above the high water mark of ordinary tides, their survival is a compliment to their sturdy construction.

After years of neglect they have been repaired on behalf of the National Trust. Only the kiln nearest the sea has been restored to its original state; the crucibles of the others have been filled and some of the kiln eyes have been blocked. But, at least, they have been preserved, and one can imagine how they once looked.

Some distance to the east at the foot of the Gribin path, surrounded by the holiday cottages of the Solva of today, is a single, towering, round kiln. Easily the largest of the surviving kilns in the locality, it was, reputedly, the last to operate; its fireplace serves as a store, while a caravan stands on its now filled crucible.

17. The Henllys kiln at Porthgain, with the modern harbour in the background.

Further on, at the bottom of Solva Hill, half hidden, is another; its former companion can only be recognised by the curve of a garden wall. Strange to think that this overgrown and inconspicuous kiln was amongst the last to work in the whole of Dewisland. It surely deserves restoration.

After Solva, the most important lime burning port in Dewisland was Porthclais. The four limekilns, in pairs, on the quays at the head of the harbour, can still be seen. Only the single kiln, some distance away on Rhoscribed land has vanished. Carefully restored by Department of the Environment stonemasons some years ago, the quayside kilns have mellowed and blended with the surroundings.

The sea-damaged kiln nearest the ocean is square, the others are round. The crucibles are all clear and the kiln eyes open. The ramps and platforms are clearly visible, the sets of steps leading to the platforms can still be climbed. Behind the western pair of kilns is the roofless limeburner's hut. Though the last coastal trader left Porthclais half a century ago, the quays and kilns have been restored to their former state. It does not require too much imagination to see the harbour as it once appeared to the youthful John Miles Thomas.

But most evocative of all must surely be the solitary, massive, square kiln at Caerbwdi. Today, it seems incredible that small sailing ships once came here, and that coal and limestone were laboriously hauled to the kiln standing on the hillside above the now-ruined mill.

The reason for its existence is that it stands on Carnwchwrn land, which

18. The kilns on the western quay at Porthclais, with the ruined limeburner's hut behind the nearer kiln.

was once the property of the bishop. So, too, were Henllys, Longhouse and Poyntz Castle, the sites of other kilns, and many of the corn mills were his. The Church itself owned the harbour at Porthclais, and the stonemasons who worked on the cathedral probably built the limekilns. And, whatever they built, they built well.

Some of the kilns have probably stood for two or three centuries. There is no reason why they should not survive for several more, as mute reminders of the time of long ago when Dewisland and other parts of Pembrokeshire were the granaries which helped to feed the fast growing population of the city of Bristol.

Pembrokeshire Limekilns; A Selection

Location	Site	Description of Kilns	Grid Ref
STEPASIDE	Ironworks	On hill above Ironworks; straight fronted row of large kilns with fairly tall rounded arches. Only true industrial kilns in county; built mid C19 for removing acid impurities present in iron ore. Restored; good condition.	SN 143073
TENBY	Salterns	At old limestone quarry opposite car park; 2 very large square draw kilns with tall rounded arches, now used as stores; condition fair but covered with ivy; need restoration. Before construction of railway embankment Ritec estuary was navigable for small craft.	SN 128006
	Kiln Park	At Blackrock Quarries; two straight fronted groups, each consisting of 6 very large draw kilns. Originally served by branch from Pembroke & Tenby Railway. Early C19. Eastern group has individual tall pointed arches at end and in sides. Good condition. Western group has tunnel running length of kilns, originally for direct loading of railway wagons; small rounded arches in side. Good condition.	SN 122001 SN 120001
CALDEY I.	Priory Bay	At quarry beside track to Priory; medium sized square kiln. Good condition.	SS 140968
MANORBIER		Alongside road to Park Farm; medium sized round kiln. Overgrown and partly collapsed.	SS 064981
STACKPOLE QUAY	Quarry	At entrance to quarry; large square draw kiln with fairly small, almost square arches, culm only imported. Well restored, good condition.	SR 993958
FRAINSLAKE		On track from beach near old cottage; medium sized square kiln. On MOD land, Restored by National Park Authority.	SR 903975
WEST ANGLE		On low cliff above north end of beach, medium sized round kiln. Partly collapsed, only one arch survives.	SM 853033

Location	Area	Description	Grid Ref
GOLDBOROUGH PILL		West side at head of creek; large square kiln. Crucible open; good condition, partly ivy-covered.	SM 944012
PEMBROKE	Common	Near old tidal limit below Town Wall, medium sized round kiln, arches similar to coastal kilns. Good condition.	SM 985013
LANDSHIPPING QUAY		At north end of quay; fairly large round kiln, eye having vertical sides and flat arched top. Good condition, forms part of garden.	SN 009109
HAVERFORDWEST	Cartlett	No remains of actual kilns, but Lower Prospect Place served as loading platform. In 1840 as many as 10 kilns in row.	SM 956158
LITTLE MILFORD		South of stream, short distance above footbridge, medium sized round kiln, wide eye with vertical sides, shallow rounded arch. Good condition.	SM 967119
NEYLAND	Church Lake	At roadside opposite bridge; fairly small square kiln; unusual single eye, shallow rounded arch. Restored, well preserved.	SM 959052
MILFORD	Castle Pill	West side of inlet near boatyard below Black Bridge; fairly large round kiln. Overgrown, fair condition.	SM 914061
	Priory Pill	West side of Pill alongside footpath; almost totally collapsed. On opposite side of stream is medium sized round kiln in fair condition.	SM 902072
SANDY HAVEN		About 100 yds east of chapel; small square kiln; almost rectangular eye. Well restored, private property.	SM 857087
		West side at head of lane; fairly large round kiln with tapered arch; nearby weighbridge & hut for burner. Whole complex well restored.	SM 853074
DALE	Pickleridge	Beside road; pair of medium sized round kilns of typical coastal design. Overgrown but in good structural condition.	SM 808066
	Castlebeach	Just above beach; small single round kiln & nearby remains of limeburner's hut. Partly collapsed, poor condition.	SM 818051
SKOMER I.	North Haven	Near top of path from landing place; medium sized square kiln. Good condition. Remains of earlier kiln nearby.	SM 734095
ST. BRIDE'S		Near head of bay; single medium sized round kiln with unusual rounded brick arches. Crucible filled, otherwise good condition.	SM 802109

MILL HAVEN		At head of bay; single round kiln. Poor condition, partly collapsed, largely covered in ivy.	SM 817123
NEWGALE		Alongside coast road; small round kiln with relatively tall pointed eye. Good condition.	SM 851217
PORTH MYNAWYD		Near coast path just west of footbridge; small round kiln. Poor condition, Completely overgrown by gorse.	SM 827233
GWADN		Alongside track to St. Elvis Farm, 50 yds from beach; remains of small round kiln. Rare example of earth and stone kiln.	SM 803238
SOLVA	Harbour	East side of harbour; group of 4 fairly large round kilns (1-4 on plan) just above tideline, together with base of hut. Well restored, though only kiln nearest sea has open crucible.	SM 805242
	Lower Solva	At foot of Gribin footpath; round kiln, largest in area (5). Good condition though eyes used as stores.	SM 806243
	Lower Solva	Near Solva Bridge; fairly large round kiln (6) originally one of pair. Fair condition, though needs attention.	SM 807245
CAERBWDI		On slope above ruined mill; large square kiln with typical Dewisland eyes. Good condition though overgrown; needs some attention.	SM 767244
PORTHCLAIS	Harbour	On east (Porthclais) quay; non-identical pair. square kiln (1) nearer sea incomplete, round kiln (2) in good condition. Group well restored	SM 742242
	Harbour	On west (Porthllisky) quay; pair of fairly large round kilns (3,4), with ramps and steps. Excellent condition with ruined hut above kilns.	SM 741242
ABEREIDDI		At southern end of beach; small round kiln built from black slate. Poor condition, in urgent need of attention.	SM 797313
		In village; small round slate kiln; partly obscured, incorporated in store. Fair condition.	SM 798313
PORTHGAIN	Harbour	North of old brickworks; fairly large round kiln, predates modern harbour. Good condition, crucible part of garden.	SM 814326

ABERCASTLE	Harbour	On western side of harbour; medium sized round kiln with limeburner's hut nearby. Good condition but requires preservation.	SM 852337
ABERBACH		Beside track 100 yds from beach; small round kiln. Fair condition but overgrown. Second similar kiln nearby is totally overgrown.	SM 884351
FISHGUARD	Slade	Near shore; pair of round kilns of unequal size due to nature of site. Crucibles filled to form garden. Good condition but threatened by trees.	SM 959373
	Musland	South of river 100 yds above bridge; large round kiln. Completely overgrown, urgently needs attention.	SM 963369
PWLLGWAELOD		South of Sailor's Safety; medium sized round kiln. Fair condition though crucible filled.	SN 006398
ABERFOREST		Near head of bay; Single round kiln with tapered arches. Fair condition but needs attention.	SN 026398
NEWPORT	Parrog	On west side of quay; irregular shaped pair of kilns. One fairly large round kiln well restored together with adjacent cottage; second kiln smaller, largely covered in rubble. Owing to level nature of ground, none of 4 kilns originally on quay was built against a bank.	SN 052397
	Bryncyn	On north side of estuary about 100 yds west of bridge; large round kiln with tall pointed arches. Good condition, recently restored.	SN 062397
CEIBWR		On approach lane to beach; remains of medium sized round kiln with tall pointed arch. Partly collapsed, only one arch survives.	SN 109457
CILGERRAN	Castle	Inside castle; probably C12, small round kiln – base only survives. Oldest kiln site known in county.	SN 195431

The above list consists mainly of kilns which survive alongside the coastal path; most are readily visible and are in reasonable condition. It is not intended to be a list of all surviving kilns. Inland kilns are not (with one or two exceptions) included. A complete list of kilns in existence in 1907 is contained (in map form) in *Pembrokeshire Sea-Trading Before 1900* by Barbara George. A survey of the coastal limekilns extant between Aberystwyth and Haverfordwest in 1992 is to be found in *Coastal limekilns in south-west Wales and their Conservation* by R. Moore-Colyer.

Bibliography

EDWARDS, Sybil: 'People of the Old Port', *Pembrokeshire Magazine*, No.58, (Haverfordwest, 1988).
FENTON, Richard: *A Tour through Pembrokeshire*, (Brecon, 1811).
FRANCIS, Mary: *Lime and Pembrokeshire*, (ms., Haverfordwest Reference Library, 1931).
GEORGE, Barbara: *Pembrokeshire Sea-Trading Before 1900*, (London, 1964).
GREEN, Francis: 'Dewisland Coasters in 1751', *West Wales Historical Records*, VIII, (Carmarthen, 1919).
GREEN, Francis: Collected Papers, (Haverfordwest Reference Library).
HASSALL, C.: *General View of the Agriculture of the County of Pembroke*, (London, 1794).
HOWELLS, B. E. & K. A.: *The Extent of Cemais, 1594*, (Haverfordwest, 1977).
JAMES, David W.: *St. David's and Dewisland*, (Cardiff, 1981).
JENKINS, J. Geraint: *The Maritime History of Dyfed*, (Cardiff, 1982).
JONES, Francis: 'Bowen of Pentre Ifan and Llwyngwair', *The Pembrokeshire Historian*, No.6, (Haverfordwest, 1979).
JONES, W. B. & FREEMAN, E.A.: 'Liber Communis', *History & Antiquities of St. David's*, (London, 1856).
LEWIS, E. A.: *Welsh Port Books 1550-1603*, (London, 1927).
LEWIS, Samuel: *Topographical Dictionary of Wales*, (London, 1833).
MOORE-COLYER, R. J.: 'Of Lime and Men', *Welsh History Review*, 14, (1988).
MOORE-COLYER, R. J.: 'Limeburning in south-west Wales', *Folk Life*, 28, (1989-90).
OWEN, George: *The Description of Pembrokeshire*, (London, 1892).
PIGOT: *Commercial Directory of South Wales*, (London, 1836).
THOMAS, John Miles: *Looking Back*, (Carmarthen, 1977).
WARBURTON, F. W.: *History of Solva*, (London, 1944).
WILLIAMS, Samuel: Letter Books, etc., (NLW Aberystwyth).
WILLIS-BUND, J. W. (ed): *The Black Book of St. David's*, (London, 1902).

Map Book of Possessions of the Bishop of St. David's, 1815, (NLW Aberystwyth).
Tithe Maps, 1840, (NLW Aberystwyth, Haverfordwest Record Office).
Ordnance Survey Maps, 25 Inches to 1 Mile; First Edition, 1887; Second Edition, 1906.